Native American Tribes: The History and Culture of the Sioux

By Charles River Editors

An Oglala Lakota teepee

About Charles River Editors

Charles River Editors was founded by Harvard and MIT alumni to provide superior editing and original writing services, with the expertise to create digital content for publishers across a vast range of subject matter. In addition to providing original digital content for third party publishers, Charles River Editors republishes civilization's greatest literary works, bringing them to a new generation via ebooks.

Sign up here to receive updates about free books as we publish them, and visit Our Kindle Author Page to browse today's free promotions and our most recently published Kindle titles.

Introduction

Illustration depicting the funeral scaffold of a Sioux chief

The Sioux

"They made us many promises, more than I can remember. But they kept but one--They promised to take our land...and they took it." – Red Cloud

From the "Trail of Tears" to Wounded Knee and Little Bighorn, the narrative of American history is incomplete without the inclusion of the Native Americans that lived on the continent before European settlers arrived in the 16th and 17th centuries. Since the first contact between natives and settlers, tribes like the Sioux, Cherokee, and Navajo have both fascinated and perplexed outsiders with their history, language, and culture. In Charles River Editors' Native American Tribes series, readers can get caught up to speed on the history and culture of North America's most famous native tribes in the time it takes to finish a commute, while learning interesting facts long forgotten or never known.

On a brutally cold, late December day in 1890, the Lakota Sioux chiefs Big Foot and Spotted Elk, along with nearly 350 haggard followers, surrendered to U.S. government authorities at the Pine Ridge Reservation. Most of the Miniconjou and Hunkpapa Lakota with the two chiefs were women and children, whose male relatives and/or husbands had been slain in combat with the U.S. Army, now in a concerted effort to end the Ghost Dance. The Army had marked Big Foot for arrest, and his band had danced passionately and earnestly, hoping to achieve the promises the Ghost Dance movement offered. No doubt, their primary hope was the return of their warrior husbands and family members and the reestablishment of vast buffalo herds on the plains, which had become increasingly rare. After being escorted to Wounded Knee Creek and establishing a camp there, the Lakota were massacred the following morning by U.S. Army troops seeking to disarm them. Nearly 300 of the Native Americans in the camp were killed by the advancing troops, many while fleeing. The vast majority of the dead were women and children.

The Wounded Knee Massacre is but one event in the long and often violent history of the Sioux, one of the best known Native American tribes and participants in some of the most famous and notorious events in American history. The history of the Sioux is replete with constant reminders of the consequences of both their accommodation of and resistance to American incursions into their territory by pioneering white settlers pushing further westward during the 19th century. Some Sioux leaders and their bands resisted incoming whites, while others tried to accommodate them, but the choice often had little impact on the ultimate outcome. Crazy Horse, who was never defeated in battle by U.S. troops, surrendered to them in 1877, only to be bayoneted to death by soldiers attempting to imprison him. Black Kettle, who flew a large American flag from his lodge to indicate his friendship with the white man, was shot to death by soldiers under George Custer's command in 1868. Throughout the 19th century, the U.S. government and its officials in the West adopted a policy of dividing the Sioux into two groups: "Treaty Indians" and "Non-treaty Indians." Often they used these groups against each other or used one group to influence another, but the end was always the same. They were forced off the land where they resided, their populations were decimated by disease, and they were forced onto reservations to adopt lifestyles considered "appropriate" by American standards.

Despite being one of the most erstwhile foes the U.S. government faced during the Indian Wars, the Sioux and their most famous leaders were grudgingly admired and eventually immortalized by the very people they fought. Sitting Bull and Crazy Horse remain household names due to their leadership of the Sioux at the fateful Battle of the Little Bighorn, where the native warriors wiped out much of George Custer's 7th Cavalry and inflicted the worst defeat of the Indian Wars upon the U.S. Army. Red Cloud remains a symbol of both defiance and conciliation, resisting the Americans during Red Cloud's War but also transitioning into a more peaceful life for decades on reservation.

Native American Tribes: The History and Culture of the Sioux comprehensively covers the culture and history of the Sioux, profiling their origins, their famous leaders, and their lasting legacy. Along with pictures of important people, places, and events, you will learn about the Sioux like you never have before, in no time at all.

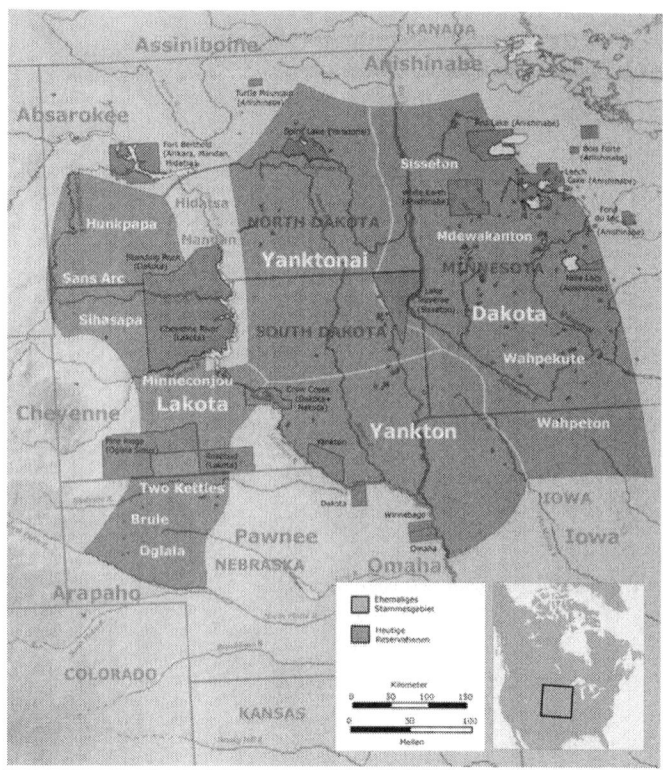

Sioux Lands in the 18th century are depicted in green. Today's reservations are depicted in orange.

Native American Tribes: The History and Culture of the Sioux
About Charles River Editors
Introduction
   Chapter 1: Origins of the Sioux
   Chapter 2: The Arrival of Wasichu and Red Cloud's War
   Chapter 3: The Start of the Great Sioux War
   Chapter 4: The Battle of the Little Bighorn
   Chapter 5: The Aftermath of Little Bighorn
   Chapter 6: The Wounded Knee Massacre and Modern Sioux History

Chapter 1: Origins of the Sioux

Traditional Lakota womendress

It is probable that the Sioux people originally lived in the present-day southeastern United States and migrated from that area northward during a warm period that occurred between the 11th and 14th centuries. Sioux languages are related to Native American languages from the present-day southeastern United States, and they were possibly part of the Mississippian (Mound Builders) culture. The tribe settled in the Midwest (modern Ohio) before moving farther north to present-day Minnesota.

Originally the Sioux had been farmers who primarily grew squash and beans, but the change in climate and their new environment forced them to abandon an agricultural lifestyle for hunting and gathering. More importantly, the Sioux found themselves surrounded by large and powerful tribes after settling in this new area. From the Minnesota region, the bulk of the tribe was pushed farther west into the present-day Dakotas by the Ojibwa tribe, though the Isanti (Santee Sioux) remained in the region. Unlike most indigenous peoples, who tended to advance from nomadic lifestyles to sedentary ones, the Sioux abandoned an agricultural existence for the nomadic life of hunting and gathering.

After being forced out of the Minnesota area, the greater tribe was split into three sub-groups. The Santee Sioux mentioned above remained in southern, present-day Minnesota and was the easternmost band of the tribe. The Yanktonai (Yankton or Western Dakota) settled in present-day southern South Dakota and were among the bands to meet Lewis and Clark and the Corps of Discovery in 1804. The Teton or Lakota – the largest and eventually the most powerful band of Sioux – settled in present-day northwestern Nebraska and eastern Wyoming.

In addition to these major divisions, each subgroup was divided into multiple bands. The Santee were composed of four bands: the Mdeakantonwon, the Wahpeton, the Wahpekute, and the Sisseton. The Yankton Sioux were divided into three bands: the Yankton, the Upper Yankton, and the Lower Yankton. Finally, the Lakota were composed of seven bands: the Oglala, the Sicangu or Brule, the Hunkpapa, the Miniconjou, the Sihasapa, the Itazipacola or Sanas Arc (Without Bows), and the Oohenupa or Two Kettles. Each band occupied its own territory within the greater territory of the sub-group and each band felt inextricably tied to that territory as a part of the land. During certain times of the year, several or all the bands of a subgroup might meet for celebrations or religious ceremonies.

As the various Sioux bands came into contact and conflict with Europeans, white settlers, and eventually the U.S. military, all of them failed to understand the reverence Native Americans held for their traditional territory, instead holding distinctly Eurocentric ideas about land ownership and property in general. Sioux foundational narratives illustrate both the attachment to place held by indigenous people of the Great Plains and their vision of themselves as vital components of their environment. The White Buffalo Woman story (shared by all Sioux and other tribes who relied on the buffalo for their survival) and the Lakota Creation story offer explanations for specific beliefs and the ideals Sioux people should strive to embody.

The Lakota Creation story, like most creation stories, is replete with fantastic scenes that serve to explain and establish aspects of life for the Sioux. Also called the Wind Cave story, the myth centers around the themes of marriage, child birth, and infidelity. At the beginning of the story, the Lakota gods are described as living in a celestial kingdom while humans were living in an uncultured state underground. Other gods are introduced during the story, including a key character in nearly all such myths, the trickster, in this case Inktomi ("spider"). The Earth seems to have already existed and the "creation" in this story seems more about bringing humans to the surface and establishing Lakota culture.

The Wind Cave story seeks to explain *why things are the way they are*. As the story opens, the chief god, Takushkanshkan (literally "something that moves," referring to the Sun) and the

Moon are married and have a daughter named Wohpe ("falling star"). Old Man and Old Woman also have a daughter who is married to Wind and has four sons by him, the Four Winds. The daughter's name is Ite ("face"). The devious trickster, Inktomi, in a bid to improve Ite's status, arranged an illicit liaison between her and Takushkanshkan. The conspiracy, which involved Old Man and Old Woman, resulted in another child named Wamniomni ("whirlwind"). When Moon discovered the affair, Takushkanshkan punishes the others involved. Old Man and Old Woman are banished to the Earth, and Ite is forcibly divorced from her husband, Wind. Along with his four sons and Wamniomni, Wind creates space. Wohpe is also cast down to the Earth and later lives with the symbol of Lakota maleness, the South Wind, and the couple adopts Wamniomni.

Takushkanshkan separates Moon from himself and gives her a domain of her own. The separation causes the creation of time.

On the Earth, the fallen gods grow increasingly bored, and eventually, Ite convinces Inktomi to find her people Tatanka Oyate (the "Buffalo Nation"). After transforming himself into a wolf, Inktomi travels through the underworld and finds a human settlement. After describing the wonder of the Earth, Inktomi is able to convince one man, Tokahe ("the first"), to journey to the surface with him. The two reach the surface through a cave (traditionally believed to be Wind Cave in the Black Hills), and Tokahe is impressed by the beauty of the green grass and the blue sky. Together, Inktomi and Ite introduce the man to buffalo meat and instruct him in making teepees, clothes, and hunting. Tokahe returns to his underworld village and convinces another six men and their families to venture to the surface with him, citing the wonders there. However, Inktomi has tricked the men, and they are soon starving. The buffalo are scarce, and the weather is bad. Also, the men cannot return to their homes; they are trapped on the surface. Using the new technologies they have learned about, these first men are able to survive and become the founders of the "Seven Hearths," a confederation of the seven bands of the Lakota.

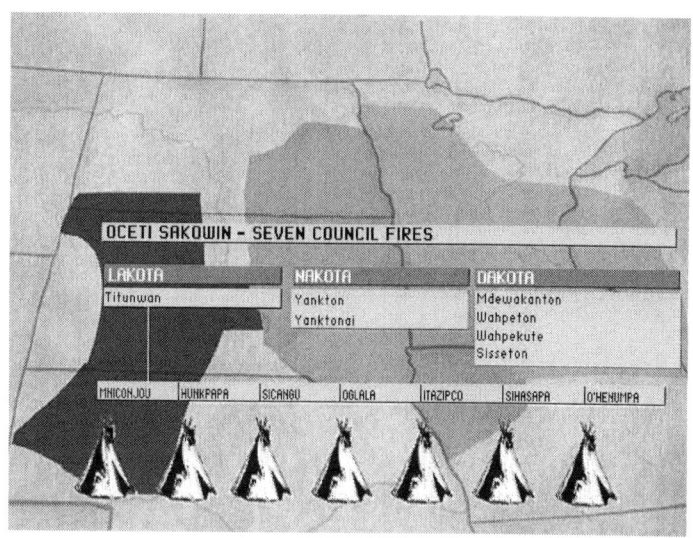

The Lakota creation narrative serves to explain the source of the buffalo as a provider of virtually all of the Sioux's needs and explains the genesis of one of their council organizations, the Seven Hearths. It also establishes and explains the sacred nature and importance of the Black Hills to the Sioux and illustrates the sacred status of buffalo and hunting. The consequences of sexual immorality is shown by the results of the affair between Takushkanshkan and Ite; their offspring, Wamniomni, is the whirlwind or tornado, a destructive, chaotic, and unpredictable natural phenomenon. In that sense, the Lakota creation myth serves as a morality tale, an explanation of the Sioux's origins, and an example of why the Black Hills are sacred to the Sioux.

The Lakota came to rely on the buffalo as their main food source, but they also considered the animals sacred, and the bulls were considered a kind of beast-god capable of delivering messages to Lakota people. The animal also features prominently in the most important Lakota religious narrative, White Buffalo Woman. The story of White Buffalo Woman is central to Lakota faith, and it establishes both the buffalo as a sacred animal and the lives Lakota people ought to pursue.

The White Buffalo Woman narrative says that in the days before the Lakota had horses, when food was scarce and difficult for the Lakota to obtain, two hunters set out from camp very early and ventured onto the Plains in search of game animals. After spending some time on the Plains and finding no game, the two men saw something approaching them from a far distance. Soon, they saw that it was a woman wandering alone on the Plains. She was dressed in white and her buckskin clothing was decorated with sacred designs formed from multi-colored porcupine quills. Her long black hair flowed freely with only one strand tied with buffalo skin, and she bore a bundle on her back. Immediately, one of the hunters was overcome with lust for the woman, and he announced his intent to have his way with her. His fellow hunter tried to dissuade him, saying that it was clear that this was a holy woman. The first man would have none of it and when the woman beckoned to him once, he made up his mind and approached her. As he reached out to touch her, a cloud covered both him and the woman. When the cloud passed, the foolish man had been reduced to a pile of bones at the woman's feet, writhing with snakes.

The woman then spoke to the other hunter, instructing him to return to his people and tell his chief to build a great teepee, large enough to hold all of his people and prepare for her arrival. She said that she was coming from Tatanka Oyate (the buffalo nation) with a message for the chief's people. The young hunter ran all the way back to camp and passed on the woman's message. The chief of the band, Standing Hollow Horn, had several teepees combined into a single large one, and the people assembled, waiting in anticipation for the woman to arrive. After four days of waiting, scouts saw something beautiful approaching. Suddenly, as soon as they had seen her, the woman was inside the giant teepee, walking around it in a sunwise (clockwise) manner. She stopped before Standing Hollow Horn, on the west side of the lodge, and showed him her bundle. The woman told the chief to look on the contents of her bundle and to always love and respect them. Also, she advised him that no one who was unclean should be allowed to touch the bundle's contents.

The bundle held the cannupa and the woman explained its significance and the meaning of the signs and symbols on it. She explained to the people that the red stone of the pipe was carved in the shape of a buffalo calf and represented all of the four-legged creatures. The wooden stem of the pipe stood for all of the things growing out of the Earth, and the twelve feathers decorating the pipe stood for all the winged creatures. Additionally, the woman told the Lakota that they would walk the Earth with the cannupa; that the Earth was the Lakota's mother and grandmother, and the Plains people would be family with the growing things, the winged creatures, and four-legged creatures. Essentially, White Buffalo Woman was telling the Lakota that they were one with Mother Earth and all of her children.

Finally, she said that if the Lakota revered the cannupa and remembered their brotherhood with the animals and plants, they would prosper. After telling the Lakota that the seven circles carved on the pipe represented the seven rites, she turned back to Standing Hollow Horn and told him that she would watch his people through the four ages and would return to them at the end. She again walked sunwise around the lodge, left the teepee, walked out onto the prairie, and sat down, facing the people watching her. The Lakota watching were amazed when the woman rose and had transformed into a brown and red buffalo calf. They watched as the calf walked a bit farther out onto the plain and lay down again. When the calf rose, she had transformed into a white buffalo, which continued walking onto the plain until it was far in the distance where she rolled over and turned into a black buffalo. The black buffalo bowed to each of the four directions and disappeared over a hill.

White Buffalo Woman's visit taught the Lakota a number of things. First, the hunter who foolishly approached her in hopes of a sexual encounter had succumbed to his passions, symbolized by the snakes among his bones. If the Lakota gave in to their physical lusts, those desires would destroy them. Second, she taught the Lakota the first of the seven rites, "keeping the soul," which was a ritual that helped grieving loved ones form a "new relationship" with a deceased relative. They would learn the other rites on their own. Third, White Buffalo Woman established the buffalo as a sacred animal and the bearer of messages from Wakan Tanka. Fourth and finally, the woman assured the Lakota that she would look upon them throughout the four ages and would return to them in the end.

The story deals with morality by graphic illustrating the danger of submitting to one's carnal desires by relating the fate of the hunter with sex on his mind. While the Sioux and many Native American did not hold puritanical views regarding sexual relations, monogamy was generally the norm among them (though polygamy was acceptable often between relatives, as with a brother "adopting" his deceased sibling's wife and children for example). Sexual immorality and especially adultery were severely punished, usually by disfigurement. The sacred bundle containing the pipe shows that White Buffalo Woman established the smoking ceremony among the Sioux and advises the Sioux to revere the smoking ceremony forever. Finally, by transforming into a buffalo that has come to them as a representative of Tatanka Oyate, the narrative establishes the primary food source of the Plains peoples as sacred. Hunting becomes a sacred act, and by the late 19th century, severe penalties were meted out to hunters who violated the strict hunting codes. These rules likely concerned preserving resources and may have included things like bans on killing female buffaloes with calves or perhaps restrictions on hunting seasons. Over time, the Sioux organized formal societies, overseen by older men, which established and policed hunting and virtually all aspects of life.

The sacred nature of the buffalo is also indicated in an account that records how the legendary chief Sitting Bull received his adult name. Once, while sitting around a campfire during a hunting expedition with several other Lakota men, Returns Again and his companions heard a guttural, voice-like sound coming from nearby. Soon, they discovered that the sounds were coming from a bull buffalo that had approached their camp. The sounds continued, and Returns Again, a mystic, began to understand that the buffalo was speaking to the hunters. As the only one who understood the buffalo's words, Returns Again realized that the sacred animal was giving him a list of names he could adopt or give to others. The first of these was Sitting Bull, which the mystic immediately adopted and eventually passed on to his son as his adult name.

Sitting Bull

Sometime in the 1760s, the Sioux began obtaining horses and quickly adapted them to their nomadic lifestyles, following massive buffalo herds roaming the Great Plains. The horse cultures of the Great Plains obtained horses through trading with other tribes farther south who had obtained horses from the Spanish. Horses were re-introduced to the Americas soon after first contact, but Native Americans adopted them slowly over the course of about two centuries. During the Conquest of New Spain, Cortés had consciously sought to keep indigenous people from obtaining horses and even hid the fact that horses and riders were separate entities for as long as possible. To the Aztec and other natives who initially encountered the Spanish on horseback, it was easy for them to believe rider and horse were one terrifying creature.

Previously, it was believed that Native Americans had obtained horses by capturing animals that had escaped from the Cortés expedition, but more recent scholarship has revealed that during the late 16th and early 17th centuries, the Spanish governor of New Mexico allowed hacienda owners to employ some Native Americans on horseback to manage large ranches. However, the average Spanish settler was barred from trading horses to Native Americans. The Pueblo men employed by the ranchers sometimes left the "encomienda" system and took the horses with them. As a result, the Apache and Navajo tribes were the first to obtain horses, and the first account of a mounted Native American was a 1623 encounter between a Spanish Friar and a band of Gila Apache raiders whose war chief was mounted.

    The ban on trading horses to indigenous people continued, but by about 1640, Spanish officials were turning a blind eye to trade between Spanish colonists and Native Americans. Around the same time, Navajo and Pueblo people began to chafe under the yoke of the Spaniards and rumors of revolt began spreading. Also, some Native Americans working Spanish horses began yielding entire herds to their fellow indigenous people. By the early 18th century, the Comanche had become the middle-men in much horse trading throughout their range in the southern plains. From the present-day southwestern United States, horses worked their way through trade networks throughout the West until many tribes had mastered horsemanship and had adopted the animal completely into their ways of life. The first Sioux to obtain horses were the Lakota, who probably obtained the animals from the Arikara tribe to their west around 1760, and by 1770 white traders found horses among the Yankton and Dakota Sioux, though they had had none just two years earlier.

    The acquisition of horses did not change Sioux culture; rather, they adapted the horse to their lifestyles. Prior to the introduction of horses, Sioux used the travois (a triangular, wooden framework, loaded with goods and dragged by a draft animal) with dogs, but the horse offered the advantage of carrying hundreds of pounds on a travois. To serve the needs of the average Sioux family, 8-10 horses might be required, but these few animals replaced the sometimes 30 or more dogs needed by the same family. In addition, Native Americans were able to do everything necessary to care for and maintain their horses, freeing them from dependence on white traders and giving them a valuable item they could trade for iron goods. Indigenous people also soon surpassed most whites in horsemanship.

    For the Sioux, the horse became a prestige item, creating a class system within the tribes based on horse ownership. Horses were owned by the individual and not held collectively by the band, so warriors could improve their standing within the band by acquiring horses through raiding. A Native American man could also marry and support more than one woman by virtue of owning a sufficient number of horses, and they could afford to lend horses to less "wealthy" members of the band for camp moves or buffalo hunts, thus exhibiting the paramount virtue of Sioux society, generosity. In the end, horses did not alter Sioux ways of life but allowed them to fully and more efficiently exploit the resources available to them, mainly the buffalo. Buffalo hunting became comparatively easier as warriors were able to ride close to buffalo and run with them as they fled.

    Despite being a nomadic people, Sioux life was surprisingly regimented. Political leadership was ultimately based on the cooperation of many individuals toward the common goal of continuing the tribe's way of life. Tribal affairs were governed by a series of "societies" similar to modern fraternities or civic organizations. Leaders were chosen based upon their parentage and upon the individual's behavior, especially his bravery, generosity, wisdom, and will. Nominated leaders became members of the Naca Ominicia, a leadership society composed of elders that made decisions regarding the tribe's well being. These leaders decided when and where to conduct hunts, when to move camps, and whether to make peace or war with neighboring tribes. Two types of societies existed: Naca societies and Akicita societies. Each type served a different group of men, and each society served a specific purpose. Men joined or sought membership in such societies for much the same reason that modern men join fraternal organization or "lodges". Society membership increased a warrior's status among his band.

Akicita societies were composed mainly of younger men and served to train warriors and hunters. These societies also policed the band, reprimanding those who broke tribal law, sometimes harshly. For example, a man who broke hunting laws might have his hunting implements or teepee destroyed. Some societies dictated a warrior member's actions in battle. A member of the Strong Heart Warrior Society was privileged to wear a long red sash and obliged to choose a spot on the battlefield and stake himself there using that sash. The warrior would remain there at that spot, fighting to the death if necessary, until "released" by another Strong Heart member.

The Naca societies were composed of tribal elders who elected 7-10 men who served as leaders called Wicasa Itancan (meaning "chief man"), each of whom interpreted, established, and enforced the decisions of this society of elders. These band leaders also appointed several "Shirt Wearers" who disseminated the Naca society's decisions. Shirt Wearers served as intermediaries between arguing families and other bands, and usually hailed from leadership families from within the band. However, such provenance was not a requirement, and Crazy Horse serves as an example of a Shirt Wearer who was not born to a "noble" family. The Naca Societies also appointed a Wakincuza or "Pipe Holder," who ranked below the Shirt Wearers and were charged with regulating peace ceremonies, designating specific camp sites, and directing the Akicita Societies during hunts.

Sioux warrior and elder societies essentially dictated life and political behavior for Sioux people, but ultimately each warrior was free to move his lodge and family as he saw fit. This freedom included the ability to leave one band and join another, and it embodied the reality that, for Sioux warriors, no man could tell another what to do.

Chapter 2: The Arrival of Wasichu and Red Cloud's War

The failure of military officers and white settlers to understand the philosophy and deeply spiritual ties to the land observed by Sioux people (and Native Americans in general) led to a series of conflicts between them and whites, collectively known as the Indian Wars. This series of conflicts is generally divided into three parts: The Dakota War (1862), Red Cloud's War (1866-1868), and the Black Hills War (1876-1877). Of these conflicts, only Red Cloud's War was considered a complete Sioux success, though the United States refused to comply with agreements and concessions it made in the Treaty of Fort Laramie (1868), leading to further tension and ongoing skirmishes between white settlers and soldiers and Native Americans living in and around the Black Hills of present-day South Dakota. Throughout these wars, the attitude of the white settlers, officials, and soldiers demonstrates the complete and diametric opposition between Native American and white societies and worldviews.

The term "wasichu" is often translated simplistically as "white man," but the Lakota word actually seeks to convey a much more nuanced and defining idea. Wasichu is more likely a play on the Lakota phrase wasin-icu, meaning "to steal the fat." The word wasichu therefore likely refers to a state of mind rather than a group of people alone. Given the Native American tendency to name people according to their observed traits and the love of word play among the Lakota, it is likely that the word wasichu seeks to describe the white settlers' desire to steal all of the good things – the fat – from the Plains people. It is likely that wasichu should be considered more like the description of an attitude than a particular ethnicity or race.

During the 19th century, Native Americans living on the Great Plains engaged in warfare with rival tribes over boundary disputes involving access to hunting grounds or other resources, and this was also a way to obtain horses and thus prestige. For the Sioux, the white settlers crossing their territory represented a "new tribe" that was violating established tribal boundaries. Had only a few wagon loads of settlers passed through their territory, the Native Americans would have likely ignored the incursions, but between 1864 and 1866 over 3,500 settlers made their ways through sacred, Native American hunting grounds.

With the introduction of horses and firearms, the tenor of intertribal warfare began to change on the Plains during the early 19th century. The sheer deadliness of these new weapons had a grave impact on Plains peoples, as killing enemies became relatively easy. The availability of firearms and liquor, both provided by white settlers and traders, would culminate in an event that would greatly shape relations between the Sioux and the U.S.

In 1851, General William S. Harney convened a meeting, calling all western Sioux bands to Fort Laramie to negotiate territorial and "right-of-way" issues through their territory. U.S. officials wanted the Sioux to end intertribal warfare to achieve Harney's goal of allowing settlers to pass through the region in safety. As a result, the general was ordered to obtain permission from the Native American leaders for settlers traveling through Sioux lands en route to the Pacific coast. This became even more imperative when the California Gold Rush of 1849 led that many more people west in search of riches.

General Harney

The government solution was to assign each band a defined territory where they were to remain, but such types of negotiation were meaningless to the Sioux, who failed to see the validity made without the consensus of all involved. The Oglalas especially viewed the negotiations with suspicion and were largely uninterested in the outcome until one Oglala leader, Bear Bull, was plied with liquor and persuaded to advocate for the treaty among his fellow Oglalas. The old chief strongly argued for the treaty and even sought to dictate the actions of his people. His attempt was a complete and utter failure, and his drunken response was a rash decision to fire into a crowd of his own people, during which he killed Red Cloud's father and brother.

In the warrior societies of the Plains, it fell upon Red Cloud to avenge the deaths of his relatives, and with a stolid nature born from a knowledge of and faith in his way of life, Red Cloud challenged Bear Bull. In the ensuing challenge, Red Cloud shot and killed both Bear Bull and his son, who had tried to defend his inebriated father. While this outcome seemed harsh and tragic, Red Cloud's actions were supported by his people; he had done what was expected of an Oglala warrior.

Red Cloud

Eventually, the Fort Laramie Treaty of 1851 was signed between the Americans and representatives for several Native American tribes, including the Cheyenne, Sioux, Arapaho, Crow, Assiniboine, Mandan, Hidatsa, and Arikara. The treaty offered tribes an annuity payment to allow white settlers access to move westward across the Oregon Trail, and the treaty effectively created and defined the territory of each participating band with the intent of ending the traditional warfare between different Sioux bands. While the Native Americans consented to the creation of roads and even forts along the route, they did not consent to settlers encroaching on the lands marked for them, which would inevitably happen as the federal government turned a blind eye.

As a result of the treaty, various warriors were designated "chiefs" by the government officials drafting the document. Red Cloud's immediate action after the murders of his father and brother won him considerable standing among the Oglalas, and soon he was regularly being consulted by Man Afraid of His Horse, the Oglalas' head chief. Over the next few years, the young warrior's influence and authority among his people grew.

Meanwhile, because the Hunkpapa group of Lakota people lived and hunted north of the most often used travel routes of white settlers, Hunkpapa Chief Sitting Bull and his people had largely avoided contact with them. While there had been intermittent contact with white trappers and traders before, the 1850s saw a great increase in contact between the two, as white settlers moved into traditionally Lakota territory. The increased contact led to culture clashes that often resulted in violence, which arguably culminated in a conflict in present-day Minnesota, at a Santee Sioux reservation located on the Minnesota River.

By the mid-1850s, the Fort Laramie Treaty of 1851 had been rendered largely meaningless. Lakota and Dakota bands who were unaware of the existence of the treaty continued their traditional and annual raiding against other Native American bands, and white settlers and migrants continually trespassed through Sioux territory in violation of the treaty's stipulations.

In 1854, various Sioux bands were encamped near Fort Laramie when an emaciated cow wandered into the mixed Lakota camp where Red Cloud and Spotted Tail were living. In such mixed gatherings, Native Americans assumed a very forgiving and conciliatory attitude toward one another, a politeness that sought to avoid unnecessary conflict. A Miniconjou warrior named High Forehead soon slaughtered and processed the animal, but it turned out the bovine had escaped from a Mormon wagon train migrating west. Shortly after, the animal's owner approached Lieutenant John Fleming, the senior officer at Fort Laramie, reporting that Native Americans had stolen his cow.

Chief Spotted Tail

Fleming summoned Conquering Bear to the fort to discuss the matter, because Conquering Bear was the Brule Lakota warrior who had been arbitrarily named a "chief" by the American representatives during the Fort Laramie treaty council in 1851. They had demanded a single representative from each group with which to deal, and when the indigenous people did not acknowledge a single leader, they appointed leaders for them. When Conquering Bear arrived at Fort Laramie, he tried to negotiate compensation for the cow, offering several ponies from his personal herd or a cow from the band's herd, understanding that the conditions of the Fort Laramie Treaty rendered this matter to the Indian Agent. The Mormon migrant refused these offers and instead demanded $25, and Lieutenant Fleming gave in to the Mormon demand that the offending Native American, High Forehead, be arrested. To do so he dispatched his subordinate to the Lakota camp to arrest the offending warrior. Second Lieutenant John L. Grattan was ready and willing to lead a force to arrest High Forehead, but both he and his commander were unaware that these types of matters had been delegated to the local Indian Agent and were not the purview of the military.

A photo of Fort Laramie in the 1850s

The appointed agent had not yet arrived in the area, so on August 29, 1854, Grattan led a force of twenty-nine soldiers, interpreter Lucien Auguste, and two cannons to the Lakota encampment. Auguste was greatly disliked by the Lakota and drank heavily on the way to the camp, arriving very drunk. As the soldiers entered the camp, Auguste began taunting the warriors, calling them women and saying that the soldiers had come to kill, not to negotiate. Grattan broke Auguste's bottle and openly berated him, indicating that he likely understood the danger of the situation his force faced. The encampment was populated by an estimated 4,800 mixed Lakota people and about 1,200 warriors.

James Bordeaux, who owned the nearby trading post, was consulted and advised Lieutenant Grattan to speak directly with Conquering Bear and allow the Native American leadership to handle the situation. Although Bordeaux reported that Grattan seemed to understand, the young, recent West Point graduate went directly to High Forehead's lodge and demanded his surrender. When High Forehead refused, Grattan then went to Conquering Bear and demanded that he hand over High Forehead. The warrior refused because he had no authority over the Miniconjou and did not want to violate the tradition of hospitality extended to visitors from other bands.

The negotiations went on for some time, with the drunken Auguste speaking broken Dakota (since he had no knowledge of other dialects). As Grattan pushed Conquering Bear to hand over High Forehead, warriors moved into flanking positions around the soldiers. Exasperated, Grattan ended the discussion and began walking back to his column. As he walked, one of the nervous troops fired a shot that struck a Lakota warrior. Chaos ensued and a firefight broke out, during which Conquering Bear was shot in the back and died nine days later. Grattan, Auguste, and the rest of the soldiers were soon dead. As the fight progressed a group of about eighteen soldiers tried to break out and reach the safety of some nearby rocks, but they were run down and killed by a group of warriors led by Red Cloud. The enraged Native Americans then looted the trading post but did not hurt Bordeaux, whom they regarded as a friend.

In the aftermath of what newspapers would call the Grattan Massacre, the massive Native American camp disbanded and left for their respective hunting grounds. The army sent a reprisal force into Lakota territory the following year, and though Crazy Horse's band was spared from them, the youth witnessed their effects, seeing Lakota teepees and possessions that had been burned by a force of some 600 troops led by General William S. Harney. The incident was referred to as the Battle of Ash Creek and resulted in the deaths of some 85 Lakota people. Soon after this massacre, the Lakota began to call Harney "Woman Killer."

The "Grattan Massacre" had become a catalyst for a generalized hostility between whites and Lakota people that would last for over two decades, but despite the obvious implications of the Grattan Massacre, at first there was no real reaction or retribution from the U.S. Army and government. Intertribal warfare between Sioux bands and their Cheyenne and Arapaho enemies resumed around 1860, but it was not until after 1862, when Union Pacific Railroad workers began surveying a route through the southern buffalo hunting grounds, that trouble arose. The Native Americans relied on summer buffalo hunts and feared that the railroad running directly through their southern hunting grounds would disrupt the annual hunt. Numerous Plains people of many different tribes met at these southern hunting camps during the annual summer hunt, and despite current animosities they met together to celebrate feasts and to hold joint councils. Increasingly, these councils were concerned with their common enemy, and intertribal rivalries were put aside. During the joint councils, Red Cloud spoke strongly against any submission to the continuing government demands for the end of intertribal warfare. Just prior to the attack on Fort Kearney in 1866, Red Cloud addressed a group of Dakotas, saying:

"When the Great Father at Washington sent us his chief soldier [General Harney] to ask for a path through our hunting grounds, a way for his iron road to the mountains and the western sea, we were told that they wished merely to pass through our country, not to tarry among us, but to seek for gold in the far west. Our old chiefs thought to show their friendship and good will, when they allowed this dangerous snake in our midst. They promised to protect the wayfarers. Yet before the ashes of the council fire are cold, the Great Father is building his forts among us. You have heard the sound of the white soldier's ax upon the Little Piney. His presence here is an insult and a threat. It is an insult to the spirits of our ancestors. Are we then to give up their sacred graves to be plowed for corn? Dakotas, I am for war!"

Less than a week after this speech, the Native American attack that would be known as the Fetterman Massacre was launched by a mixed Sioux force. In the summer of 1866, Colonel Henry B. Carrington set out from Fort Laramie to establish a series of forts along the Bozeman Trail with the goal of protecting migrants moving along the trail. The Bozeman Trail ran through the Powder River country, which included the traditional hunting grounds of Lakota, Cheyenne, and Arapaho peoples. Carrington had about 1,000 people in his column, of which about 700 were soldiers and 300 were civilians, likely soldiers' families and migrants.

Carrington

The Colonel established Fort Phil Kearny as his headquarters and based 400 troops and most of the civilians there. During the construction of Fort Kearny, which lasted months, Native

Americans killed several dozen soldiers and civilians in some fifty separate attacks. The attacks were largely focused on the "wood trains", comprised of soldiers and civilians harvesting lumber from the surrounding forest for the construction of the fort. Though younger warriors like Crazy Horse conducted the actual attack, Red Cloud and other, older leaders would help plan and direct the harassment and interdiction campaign against the construction of Fort Kearney.

By October 1866, Carrington's officers and men pressured him to go on the offensive and take the fight to the Native Americans. The pressure was increased by the arrival of a company of sixty-three cavalry troopers led by Lieutenant Horatio S. Bingham in early November. Civil War veterans Captain William J. Fetterman and Captain James W. Powell accompanied the cavalry troopers and were assigned to Fort Kearny as infantry officers, but despite having a distinguished war record, Fetterman had no experience fighting Native Americans. Nevertheless, that lack of experience did not keep Fetterman from criticizing the conservative and defensive posture Carrington had established at Fort Kearny, adding to an already growing chorus of criticism. Fetterman also repeatedly displayed utter contempt for the Native Americans.

In late November, Carrington received orders from his commander, General Philip St. George Cooke, to take the offensive against the Native Americans. The first opportunity for offensive action came on December 6, when pickets reported that a wood train four miles from the fort was under attack. The attack was however, merely a feint, meant to lure troops into a Native American ambush. Carrington ordered Fetterman to take a company of cavalry, bolstered by a squad of mounted infantry, to relieve the wood train. Meanwhile, Carrington would lead a mounted squad to the north to cut off the Native Americans' presumed escape route.

As Carrington moved to cut off his enemies' retreat, several men became separated from the group, and the reduced party soon found itself surrounded by about 100 mounted warriors. Fetterman arrived just in time rescue Carrington's small force and the warriors retreated. Soon afterwards, one of the men who had been separated appeared fleeing for his life before seven warriors. The other men with him had been killed, and troops found their bodies later that day. Carrington and Fetterman were both deeply affected by the incident, and the Colonel stepped up training for his soldiers to improve their discipline, reorganized his command into six companies, and doubled the number of guards accompanying the wood trains. The commander also ordered that the remaining 50 horses (the rest had been lost to Native American raids) be kept saddled and ready to venture forth at a moment's notice from dawn until dark.

On December 19, another wood train was attacked, and Carrington dispatched a mixed company of cavalry and mounted infantry led by Captain Powell. This time, the cautious officer followed Carrington explicit orders not to pursue the Native Americans over the ridge and out of sight of the fort. Powell was successful and returned to the fort unscathed. Carrington continued to emphasize the need for caution until reinforcements and horse arrived from Fort Laramie.

Two days later, Native Americans again attacked a wood train, and Carrington dispatched a mixed force of about 50 infantrymen and nearly 30 cavalry troopers and Colonel Carrington again chose Captain Powell to lead the relieving force, but Fetterman asserted his seniority to Powell and was thus given command of the soldiers. Again, Carrington ordered the troops not to pursue the warriors over the nearby ridge and out of sight of the fort.

When Fetterman left the fort, he immediately disobeyed orders and took the trail that followed the ridgeline. The Colonel assumed that Fetterman was planning to attack the warriors from the north; instead, he and his force disappeared over the ridge. At this point the attack on the wood train ended and about 50 warriors attacked the fort but were repelled by a few cannon shots.

Meanwhile, the Native American warriors had deployed a group of decoying riders, including Crazy Horse, who lured Fetterman's troops over the ridge and into the waiting ambush. About midday, soldiers at Fort Kearny heard a large volume of gunfire coming from the north, the direction where Fetterman had led his troops. Carrington dispatched 75 troops towards the gunfire and soon afterwards sent another 48. About an hour later, as the troops topped the ridgeline, they saw a group of some 1,000 warriors in the valley below. Warriors approached and taunted the soldiers, but soon they began to disperse and disappear. Captain Ten Eyck, leading the relief force, cautiously moved onto the battlefield and found Fetterman and his men dead, stripped, and mutilated. Until that time, the Fetterman Massacre, as U.S. newspapers labeled the event, was the greatest defeat (in terms of the number of U.S. soldiers killed) experienced by the Army at the hands of Native American warriors.

As the Fetterman Massacre made clear, the mode of war among Native Americans was never the organized, set-piece battle that most U.S. Army officers had been trained to fight. Rather, Native Americans usually engaged in low-intensity, raiding and other guerilla activity, and combat between Native Americans was not always lethal. Crazy Horse was known for sometimes venturing into battle with only his *coup stick*–a narrow, decorated wand. Being slapped or struck by an enemy with a coup stick served as a way for the attacker to say, "I could have killed you." Striking an enemy warrior with a coup stick was a sign of courage, honored among the tribes. However, once it became clear that U.S. soldiers neither carried nor honored the traditions embodied by the coup stick, their Sioux enemies opted for lethal weapons, but their tactics never changed.

The following summer, after conducting their annual Sundance Ritual, the Oglala Lakota and Cheyenne peoples formed a large settlement located on the Tongue River and Rosebud Creek. The warriors assembled, led by Red Cloud, decided to destroy Fort C.F. Smith and Fort Kearny and end the use of the Bozeman Trail. Between 500-800 warriors assembled and began moving towards Fort Smith, while the remainder struck out for Fort Kearny.

As the force approaching Fort Kearny neared it objective, they encountered a wood train and a force of 28 troops defending the train led by Captain James Powell. The Lakota warriors, led by

Crazy Horse and Hump, and the Cheyenne, led by Little Wolf, immediately attacked. Powell formed the fourteen wagons composing the wood train into an oval and the small force took shelter within. The warriors repeatedly attacked the soldiers and woodcutters in a battle that lasted over five hours. Powell's troops had recently been issued Springfield Model 1866 "Trapdoor" rifles, whose reloading time was much faster than the muzzleloaders the soldiers had previously carried. In contrast with the muzzleloaders, which could fire about three times per minute, the new .50 caliber rifles could fire ten times per minute. The Native American warriors had timed their previous attacks to coincide with the relatively long reloading time for muzzle-loading rifles, but in this case, the strategy backfired. Eventually, a relief force from Fort Kearny arrived and the warriors withdrew. Casualty estimates indicate that about 60 Native Americans were killed and twice that number wounded, while only five soldiers were killed and two wounded.

Although this last battle was hardly a victory for the Native Americans, the ongoing hostilities ultimately convinced U.S. officials to head back to the negotiating table with them. As a result, Red Cloud has often been labeled the only Indian chief to win a war against the Americans.

Chapter 3: The Start of the Great Sioux War

The Santee Sioux had succumbed to U.S. government pressure and moved onto the designated reservation in 1851. In doing so, they surrendered some 24 million acres of territory to the United States, and seven years after settling on the reservation, the Santee were robbed of half of their reservation land as well. They had agreed to sell the land in return for annuity payments, but because the payment had to pass through the hands of corrupt Indian Agents, it rarely reached the Santee. Additionally, the Indian Agency attached numerous "behavioral clauses" to the payments in an effort to "civilize" the Santee, which the Native Americans seemed never able to achieve.

In late summer of 1862, Chief Little Crow of the Santee reported to government agent Thomas J. Galbraith, shouting that his people were starving while the stores destined for the Native Americans sat in storage facilities at the Indian Agency. Another Indian Agency worker, Andrew J. Myrick responded saying, "So far as I'm concerned, if they are hungry, let them eat grass, or their own dung." Angered and issuing Sioux language war cries, the Chief and his men left, but several days later, Myrick's dead body was found, his mouth stuffed full of grass.

The Santee decided that, because the U.S. military was distracted by the Civil War, the time had come for them to reclaim the land they had ceded to the United States. Military forces were rushed to Minnesota but did not arrive before the Santee had killed over 800 white settlers and had taken or destroyed a few million dollars worth of property. In the aftermath of the attacks, U.S. Army troops captured over 2,000 Santee, summarily tried them, and sentenced over 300 to death. Later, President Abraham Lincoln reviewed the list and commuted the death sentence for all but 38 warriors. Those men were executed by hanging in what still stands as the largest mass execution in U.S. history. This uprising and the following reprisal led to near constant violence between Sitting Bull's Lakota people and the U.S. Army and white settlers. Also, the Hunkpapa heard from the Santee Sioux about the reprisals by the U.S. Army from survivors who fled west into the Plains.

In early November of 1862, 303 Santee warriors were tried by court-martial, found guilty of the murder and rape of hundreds of white settlers, and sentenced to death by hanging. President Abraham Lincoln commuted the sentenced of all but 38 warriors to prison sentences, and the 38 were executed by hanging in late December. This event remains the largest single mass execution in American history. The remaining 284 warriors were sent to prison in Iowa, where more than half died. Additionally, the promised annuities that were supposed to be paid to Santee Sioux were suspended for four years, and that money was instead paid to white victims. Many Santee fled in the aftermath of the Dakota War; some journeyed north to Canada and others joined the Lakota or Yankton bands. Some were able to remain in Minnesota and exist there to this day on small reservations.

In the aftermath of the Santee Uprising, the U.S. Army began widespread and indiscriminate reprisals against any Native American band they could find, and it was during one of these poorly-aimed revenge attacks that Sitting Bull had his first encounter with U.S. Army troops. Still, despite nearly constant strife between whites and Native Americans, anecdotal and contemporary accounts describing Sitting Bull personally paint him as gentle and kind. This behavior was also extended to white settlers who farmed in his people's area. In particular, one white woman, Mrs. Fanny Kelly, was taken captive by a Hunkpapa raiding party from her Wyoming home in 1864 and described her experience. The Hunkpapa held Mrs. Kelly for five months, and during that time, she resided with Sitting Bull and his family "as a guest." She described Sitting Bull as uniformly kind and gentle to his wife and children and courteous and polite in his interactions with all others. Additionally, Mrs. Kelly stated that Sitting Bull and his wife often went without eating so that she might have food.

Following the Fetterman and Wagon Box Fights, the U.S. government entered into a treaty with Lakota and Arapaho leaders at Fort Laramie in 1868. Red Cloud was the last of the Native American leaders to sign the Fort Laramie Treaty of 1868 (not to be mistaken with the Fort Laramie Treaty of 1851), which allegedly guaranteed that the Lakota people would own the Black Hills (Paha Sapa) of South Dakota in perpetuity, and that area would be set aside for Native Americans only. Whites could not enter the territory without the express permission of the Sioux. This was essential, because the Black Hills are the "holy land" of Lakota and other indigenous peoples. In addition, the Treaty of Fort Laramie dictated that the U.S. Army would abandon forts along the Bozeman Trail.

However, because none of the chiefs could read English, the content of the treaty was merely "explained" to them, and most of the explanation consisted of lies and half truths. In reality, the treaty provided for reservations – where the Native Americans would live – and the cession of certain tribal lands to the United States. In 1870, Red Cloud traveled to New York City and Washington D.C., speaking to crowds and explaining both his people's plight and his understanding of the Treaty of Fort Laramie of 1868. It was during this trip that he became convinced that his people could never overcome the American settlers, based on their numbers and their great cities. However, his speeches in the east were sufficient to raise public awareness and led to the alteration of the original treaty. An Indian Agency was also established on the North Platte River in 1873, expressly for the Oglala Sioux. Because the Red Cloud Agency was established, the distribution of food and goods promised to Sioux bands by the Treaty of Fort Laramie of 1868 could be delivered and distributed to the Native Americans. After the establishment of the Red Cloud Agency, a group of angry warriors reacted violently to a flagpole being erected and chopped the flagpole into little pieces. The following year, the U.S. Army established Camp Robinson near the Red Cloud Agency to both protect the agency and keep a watchful eye on the Oglala.

Meanwhile, the treaty itself was broken almost immediately. When an expedition into the Black Hills led by Lieutenant Colonel George Custer discovered gold in 1874, miners flooded into the region in violation of the treaty. Lakota people, hunting within the confines of the territory promised to them by the Fort Laramie Treaty of 1868, began encountering white settlers and attacked them. In response, whites demanded protection by the U.S. Army, which had been complying with the treaty and ejected the white interlopers.

Custer

The removal of white miners had the effect of increasing political pressure on the government to open the Black Hills to mining, logging, and settlement. In May of 1875, several Lakota leaders traveled to Washington D.C. in the hope of convincing President Ulysses S. Grant to honor the treaty conditions. They were unsuccessful, and the government attempted to purchase the Black Hills for $25,000.00. Late in the fall of the same year, Grant met with Major General Philip Sheridan and Brigadier General George Crook and the three agreed to end the policy of ejecting miners and settlers. Also, the President and the generals decided to notify Native American bands not already residing on the reservation that they had until January 31, 1876, to surrender to authorities and settle on reservations. Among these "non-treaty" bands were those led by Crazy Horse and Sitting Bull. The concept of ultimatums was foreign to Native Americans, and many bands were so far from existing reservations that they would be hard pressed to make it onto reservations before the deadline had passed even if they wanted to.

After the January 31, 1876 deadline came and went, the U.S. Army sent two columns of troops under Generals George Crook and Alfred Terry and a third column commanded by Colonel John Gibbon into the region in March of 1876. The force was composed of ten companies of cavalry and two companies of infantry and was dispatched to provide protection for civilians mining in the Back Hills. However, the U.S. troops were caught in a blizzard, and the majority of them were forced to abandon their pack train. Also, the force suffered a number of frostbite casualties. General Terry's column stalled, but Crook quickly ordered Colonel Joseph J. Reynolds with six companies of cavalry. Reynolds located a Native American village consisting of about sixty-five lodges and attacked it in mid-March. The Reynolds force believed they had located and attacked the band led by Crazy Horse, but in fact, they had attacked a Cheyenne village. Prior to the attack, the village's occupants had been allied with the United States against the Lakota and other Native American bands. In fact, the Cheyenne, whose homes had been destroyed, had been rushing to the reservation in compliance with the government order. After the attack, the Cheyenne became fierce enemies of the white settlers, and Lakota followers of Sitting Bulloffered some of the Cheyenne refuge. The attack again demonstrated the inability of U.S. troops to distinguish between friend and foe among Native Americans.

George Crook

After recovering their mounts and finding the pack train, General Crook ordered the 2nd Cavalry Regiment's commander Colonel J.J. Reynolds to take three troops (companies) from his command and continue the search for the Native Americans. Reynolds ordered one company of soldiers to attack a settlement of about 100 lodges on the Tongue River. The troopers set fire to the teepees and scattered the warriors, but they were prevented from winning a clear victory by the late winter blizzard. When Native American warriors began resisting from the outskirts of the camp, Reynolds ordered a hasty retreat and pushed his force hard in an attempt to link up with General Crook. The soldiers had managed to capture a large herd of ponies belonging to the Native Americans, but the soldiers charged with guarding the captured ponies were so tired they fell unconscious, allowing warriors who had been tracking the military force to liberate the pony herd. The Native Americans made good their escape, and Reynolds would later be court-martialed for his failure to follow-through on the initial attack. Meanwhile, the Native American survivors of the battle made their way to a settlement on the Rosebud Creek, where Crazy Horse and Sitting Bull had moved their bands.

By May of 1876, all twelve companies of the 7th Cavalry Regiment had assembled at Fort Abraham Lincoln, roughly 200 miles northeast of the Black Hills. In the middle of the month, a force of over 900 troops commanded by General Terry left Fort Abraham Lincoln, and two weeks later, a second force comprised of about 1,000 troops and support personnel and over 250 Shoshone and Crow scouts rode out of Fort Fetterman, about 100 miles southwest of the Black Hills, commanded by General Crook. Around the same time, a third column of some 450 U.S. troops, led by Colonel Gibbon, departed from Fort Ellis about 400 miles away in the Montana Territory.

Gibbon

A late spring snow delayed Gibbons and his column. The three columns marched toward an area northwest of the Black Hills in search of what they considered a hostile, Native American force. They employed a strategy of convergence, each commander having an assignment, which worked in concert with the other two to culminate in an attack on the Native American force. Crook's column was to attack the Native American bands from the south, forcing them into waiting U.S. troops. The column commanded by General Terry was to attack from east, also pushing the Native Americans into the same U.S. troops who were moving into position northwest of the presumed location of the Native American settlement. Gibbon, approaching from the northwest, was tasked with intercepting Native Americans fleeing from attacks from the south and east.

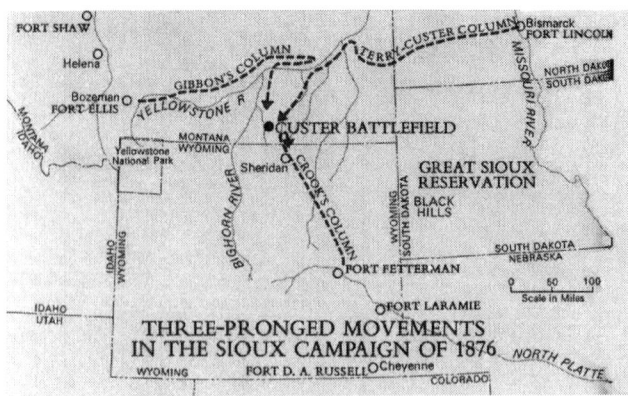

Sitting Bull held a council of Lakota that included some of the Cheyenne refugees who had escaped the Tongue River attack and said, "We must stand together or they will kill us separately. These soldiers have come shooting; they want war. All right, we'll give it to them." Some time after the council, the Lakota leader then sent couriers to every Sioux, Arapaho, and Cheyenne camp, including those who had moved onto reservations, urging them to meet him at his camp on Rosebud Creek in the Montana Territory. Responding to Sitting Bull's call, hundreds of warriors moved their families to the Rosebud Creek camp, fearing that their ancestral holy land, the Black Hills, might be lost.

Chapter 4: The Battle of the Little Bighorn

The seminal moment in George Custer's life was one that he was very nearly not a part of. In early 1876, President Grant's administration was roiled by charges of corruption, extending as far as his Cabinet members. Custer himself had to testify before Congressional hearings, which threatened to prevent him from taking a leadership position in the campaigning against the Lakota that year.

General William Tecumseh Sherman lobbied for Custer to be allowed to take command of the expedition against the Lakota from Fort Lincoln and urged new Secretary of War Alphonso Taft to request Custer's release. However, President Grant refused, instead demanding Taft have someone else lead the command. Though Custer was able to personally secure his release, he could not convince Sherman or Brig. Gen. Alfred Terry to appoint him. For his part, Sherman suggested Custer personally meet with President Grant, but when Grant refused to meet with him, Custer headed off for Chicago against the wishes of his superiors.

With Custer heading west, Sherman ordered Phil Sheridan to intercept and detain him. At this point, the expedition against the Lakota was to be headed by Major Marcus Reno. When Custer came across Brigadier General Terry at Fort Snelling, Minnesota, Terry recalled that Custer was in tears and begged him to let him lead the expedition. Terry, Sheridan, and Sherman all pressed upon Grant to let Custer lead the expedition, and Grant finally relented. In early May 1876, Custer was given command of the 7th U.S. Cavalry, under the supervision of Terry, but according to Terry's chief engineer, Captain Ludlow, Custer vowed to "cut loose" from Terry's supervision whenever he had the chance. Having been serving independent commands for years, Custer apparently did not want to play the role of subordinate.

By June the mixed group of Native American tribes had assembled into a massive army, waiting in the Rosebud Creek camp. The Native American camp eventually grew to over 10,000 people and included around 4,000 warriors. Most of the bands that had assembled in the camp were members of the Teton Sioux sub-group who had dominated a range that included the western portions of present-day North and South Dakota and extended deep into present-day Montana, Wyoming, and Nebraska. There was no acknowledged leader of the mixed bands, despite the presence of several other warriors with well-deserved reputations as great warriors, including Crazy Horse, Chief Gall, and White Bull. But one Chief commanded the respect and deference of all the warriors present: Sitting Bull.

As a holy man, Sitting Bull retreated to a lonely butte near the camp with three attendants. He took his cannupa (sacred pipe) and began to pray and smoke, saying, "Wakan Tanka save me and give me all my wild game animals. Bring them near me, so that my people may have plenty to eat." After repeating these requests, he also promised to sponsor a Sundance, his people's most revered ritual. He also vowed that during the Sundance ritual he would sacrifice a "scarlet blanket" to Wakan Tanka. The "blanket" would be composed of his own blood. Sitting Bull was asking for divine assistance in the confrontation he knew was coming or at least a portent showing how the battle would go.

It was later during the Sundance ritual, a two-day process of ritual auto-sacrifice (blood letting), prayer, and dancing, that Sitting Bull received his famous Wakan vision. For the Hunkpapa chief, the ritual started with priests painting his hands and feet red and painting blue stripes across his shoulders, representing the sky. Next came the ritual bloodletting, which involved a chosen companion picking and cutting away fifty match-head sized bits of skin from each of Sitting Bull's arms as he prayed. Soon, blood ran down both of the Chief's arms from 100 tiny cuts. Meanwhile, younger dancers had leather thongs threaded through incisions in their chests or backs. Sitting Bull then rose and began to dance in a rhythmic, hopping manner, praying as he did so. The dancing and prayer lasted all day and through the night. Periodically, the Chief gazed into the sun as it crossed through the sky. Throughout the ritual, participants neither drank nor ate but continued dancing into the following day.

Eventually, some time around noon of the following day, the ritual's climax arrived. Sitting Bull staggered a few steps and collapsed, unconscious. According to the Lakota, he had died a passing death, and as he emerged from his stupor, he had his vision. The Chief saw a mist from which he saw numerous soldiers entering the Native American camp, but they did not enter in victory. The soldiers' heads were bent in defeat, and their campaign hats were falling from their heads. He then saw them falling into the camp like so many dead grasshoppers. While the vision was encouraging, it still carried a warning and Sitting Bull would tell his people, "These soldiers are gifts of Wakan Tanka. Kill them, but do not take their guns or horses. If you set your hearts upon the goods of the white man, it will prove a curse to this nation."

After the completion of the Sundance ritual, the massive, multi-tribe group moved into an established camp in the Little Big Horn River valley. Knowing that General Crook's force was approaching, Crazy Horse and a force of about 1,000 warriors moved to engage him near Rosebud Creek.

On June 17, 1876, General Crook was leading a mixed unit of cavalry, mule-mounted infantry, teamsters, and Native American scouts (Crow and Shoshone) along the south fork of Rosebud Creek in search of Native American encampments and warriors. After the previous day's march of some thirty-five miles, Crook issued a 3:00 a.m. morning reveille and ordered the troops onward. Around 8:00 AM, Crook paused his force to rest the animals and the men. The mule-mounted infantry in particular were very tired, and despite being deep in enemy territory, Crook gave no special orders regarding the defense of the column. Troopers and civilians stopped in column order and rested where they were. Only the Native American scouts (some 250 Crow and Shoshone) remained vigilant; they ranged ahead of the column and soon the report of gunfire resounded from ahead of the troopers, growing in intensity. A scout returned to the column, shouting "Lakota, Lakota" to indicate that the Lakota were attacking.

By 8:30 AM, the scouts were fully engaged with a mixed Lakota and Cheyenne force that outnumbered them by roughly five to one. The scouts retreated to the column, and their fighting retreat allowed Crook to deploy his forces. The U.S. force found itself engaged with a Native American force that matched it in size, and the Native Americans were led by the fearsome Oglala warrior Crazy Horse, who they called Crazy Horse.

The Lakota and Cheyenne assault was initially halted when Crook ordered a cavalry charge by six platoons of cavalry commanded by Captain Anson Mills. The massed charge initially shocked the Native American warriors, who pulled back to a nearby ridgeline. Mills reformed three platoons and again charged, pushing the mixed force farther back. He was then ordered to cease his advance and set up a defensive perimeter. The commanding general also ordered his forces to seize high ground north and south of the creek, which they did.

Unfortunately for Crook, his initial charges did little damage to the Native Americans, who continued to attack the U.S. troops in small groups and fire at them from a distance. They returned and renewed their attack with such ferocity, Crook became convinced that their families must be encamped farther up the valley. Thinking he was very close to his objective, Crook ordered cavalry troopers to withdraw from the high ground and follow the creek to the north in search of the settlement.

Crook would soon miss the force he'd sent in search of the non-existent village when a detachment led by Lieutenant Colonel William Royall, a mile away from the main body of U.S. troops, came under attack by a group of Lakota and Cheyenne warriors. The warriors realized that they had the chance to cut off and destroy this group, but sensing the danger to Royall's troops, Crook sent a message to Mills, ordering him to turn on the Native American flank and relieve the pressure on Royall and his troopers. Though Mills cavalrymen arrived on the scene too late to help Royall's troopers withdraw, the Native American attack was disrupted by the unexpected appearance of Mills' cavalry troopers on their flank. An additional charge by the Crow and Shoshone scouts averted disaster for the Royall force, and the Lakota/Cheyenne force broke contact and retreated.

Crook then gathered all his mounted units and led them up the Rosebud in search of the village he was certain was there. When his cavalry column approached a narrow ravine, a perfect spot for an ambush, Crook decided to end the advance. The General led his column back to a camp on Goose Creek and waited there for seven weeks. As a result of his decision to stay at Goose Creek, Crook's force of over 1,200 men was unavailable to assist at the Battle of the Little Bighorn. His enemies, led by Crazy Horse, would go on to play pivotal roles in the coming battle just over a week later.

Though the battle did not inflict substantial damage to the U.S. troops, it was definitely a blow to their collective military psyches. Crook was reportedly shocked by the ferocity of the Lakota/Cheyenne attack and thus believed that the warriors were protecting their families, which he assumed were camping nearby. This assumption led him to split his forces and thus weaken his defense. Also, this was among the first encounters in which Native American warriors seemed willing to accept casualties during their attacks. In previous encounters, Crook had learned several things that likely tainted his expectations as he engaged the warriors at Rosebud Creek. First, Native American warriors usually avoided contact and engaged in classic guerilla tactics, hit and run or harassment and interdiction, especially when outnumbered. The U.S. commander expected this type of action at Rosebud Creek and when the warriors fought so fiercely, Crook fell into the trap of his second assumption. Crook's second assumption was his fueled by his misinterpretation of the ferocity of the Native American attack. His experiences fighting Native Americans had taught him that they only engaged in such determined attacks when they were protecting their families, and because finding Native American settlements in the area was one of his objectives, he was convinced that he had located the settlement. Third and probably most problematic for Crook, he had likely never faced a force of Native American warriors that matched his own in numbers. Related to this, Crook may have suffered from a kind of "military eugenics" complex, meaning he greatly underestimated the mental capacity and tactical combat experience of the Native American leaders. However, their tactical understanding was graphically demonstrated to him during the battle as the Native Americans quickly recognized the danger to the Royall force and exploited the opportunity.

Though General Crook claimed the battle was a U.S. Army victory, it was a hollow one, and the aftermath of the battle saw Crook withdraw his forces and wait for resupply and reinforcements at Goose Creek. As a result of his inaction, his troops were unavailable for the pending Battle of the Little Bighorn, which would take place just over a week later. In the end, Crook's force suffered light casualties, between one and three dozen killed and about forty wounded (depending on sources), but his failure to participate in the Battle of the Little Bighorn, virtually sealed the fate of the U.S. forces engaged there. Also, the Battle of the Rosebud once again demonstrated the overconfidence of U.S. troops, their officers' complete disregard for Native American leaders' competence on the battlefield, and the U.S. troopers' complete misunderstanding of the tactical realities of combat. This was exacerbated by the fact that 19th century Sioux warriors were actually among the best light cavalry in the world.

Although Crook's force had been stopped and would end up being out of the battle for all intents at purposes, General Terry and Colonel Gibbon were still approaching the Little Bighorn valley with some 1,500 mixed troops (cavalry and infantry). As stated earlier, Gibbon had been delayed from departing by the snow, and Crook's column had been stopped and was waiting at Goose Creek, but General Terry remained unaware of the misfortune that had befallen the other two columns and continued his advance. Riding in General Terry's column was the impetuous and flamboyant Lieutenant Colonel George Armstrong Custer. Custer and his 7th Cavalry Regiment, composed of roughly 600 men, were sent ahead with orders to locate the Native American encampment. The regiment was then to wait for reinforcements to move up before engaging the Native Americans.

After five years of "independent," discretionary command, on May 17, 1876, Custer and the 7th U.S. Cavalry now found themselves being just one part of what was supposed to be a coordinated two-prong attack under the Command of General Terry, Custer arrived with his 650 soldiers on the night of June 24, 1876, with the second column (under Terry) due on June 26. On June 21, Custer refused to take an additional four companies from the 2nd U.S. Cavalry, asserting that he "could whip any Indian village on the Plains" with his own men.

On the morning of June 25, Custer's scouts discovered an Indian village about fifteen miles away, in the valley of the Little Bighorn River. Choosing to disregard General Terry's orders to wait for a concerted effort, the grandstanding Custer intended to deliver his own decisive victory by dividing his command into three units, an extremely bold tactic when done in the face of a much larger force.: one under Captain Frederick W. Benteen (which he sent south to prevent the natives from escaping), one under Major Marcus A. Reno (which he sent across the river to attack the heart of the village), and one he commanded himself (which he led north and headed downstream, probably to attack a weaker point in the village).

Before the battle, it is believed Custer thought he was facing a group of about 800, which was Sitting Bull's strength in the weeks before the battle. However, the Army's Native American scouts and civilian scouts had not adequately informed the Army of the reinforcements that arrived, and at Little Bighorn, Custer's 650 men instead encountered about 2,000 highly-seasoned braves under Crazy Horse, Gall, and Sitting Bull. Allegedly, Custer disregarded the advice of his own trusted scouts, including the famous scout Bloody Knife, who insisted there were too many natives to successfully fight alone. Custer's estimation was not helped by the fact that the scouts that morning could not see many of the braves, who were still asleep in the early morning hours. Scouts had only seen some of the tribe's ponies, and Custer's own personal observations consisted mostly of tribeswomen routinely preparing for a day just like any other.

That same morning, Custer found that he was being back-trailed by Native Americans when men sent to recover supplies dropped by the column ran across two young Native Americans eating hard tack from a fallen package. The two boys had been out looking for stray horses. One of the boys was killed, but the other escaped. Additionally, as Custer's men scouted the higher ground, they found fresh pony tracks leading to vantage points above them. Custer anticipated that his attack would take the Native Americans by surprise, but when he learned that some of them had discovered trails left by his troopers, he decided to attack without delay on June 25.

Unbeknownst to the attacking troopers, the Native American boy who had earlier escaped ran into the village and warned the Native Americans just before the attack began. When the alarms were raised, Crazy Horse quickly rallied the sleeping warriors. Meanwhile, Sitting Bull was in the council lodge, and he rose and rushed to his family teepee to retrieve his personal weapons, a .45 caliber revolver and an 1873 model Winchester carbine. His nephew One Bull joined him, and the pair mounted their warhorses and rode toward the attacking Reno force to the south. However, they were preceded by a massive charge of roughly 1,000 Lakota, Teton, and Cheyenne warriors.

The first attacks of the battle began with Reno's troops, who Custer ordered to give battle, figuring the Native Americans would flee the encampment and take off. Reno's men advanced northwest toward the encampment, with both the village and his advance masked by trees. When Reno advanced into a clearing within a few hundred yards, he began to realize the actual size of the encampment, and believed the Indians had set a trap. Reno's men dismounted and formed a skirmish line, requiring a quarter of his men to hold all the horses. As they began firing at the village, the Native American warriors rushed out to attack them, outnumbering the American cavalrymen by about five to one. Eventually, the pressure on Reno's flanks forced a disorderly retreat to the east.

Sitting Bull watched as Reno's men began to fall, and within a few minutes he had concluded that he wasn't needed in the battle. Later the Chief would say, "there were plenty of warriors to meet them." As the forces led by Crazy Horse, White Bull, and Chief Gall began to push Reno's men into retreat back across the river, One Bull urged his horse into the stream in pursuit. Sitting Bull stopped him, saying they needed to prepare against an Army counter attack. The two men returned to the encampment and Sitting Bull prepared to keep his family safe.

Reno's retreat brought the scattered remnants of his men into conjunction with the detachment under Captain Benteen around 4:00 p.m. Benteen's column had been riding north on a scouting mission and was supposed to ride forward to meet Custer's column, which was farther north. And though the distinct and loud sounds of gunfire were erupting north of them, Benteen instead opted to help reinforce Reno's badly beaten men. Together, the men hastily tried to dig defensive entrenchments, which had become a routine during the later years of the Civil War, and they went about forming a rifle pit on what is now known as Reno Hill. These men held a defensive position as they were surrounded and fired upon on all sides by the warriors.

An hour later, Captain Thomas Weir, in charge of Company D, decided to attempt to reach Custer's column. Company D advanced to Weir Ridge, at which point they could make out some of the warriors on horseback shooting into the ground, presumably killing off wounded men or those who had surrendered. It remains unclear whether Weir and his men witnessed the final gasps of Custer's Last Stand, or whether it was part of the fight.

After chasing Reno's and Benteen's bloodied troops for most of the day, the Native warriors broke off the attack and dispersed, unable to fully penetrate the defenses.

1876 illustration of Custer's Last Stand

Custer, of course, suffered a different fate, one that will forever remain controversial and not completely known. What is known is that Custer's column, about 210 men, were engaged by the warriors about 3.5 miles north of Reno Hill, presumably during the time the loud gunfire could be heard by the men digging in on Reno Hill. When General Terry arrived and the site of Custer's Last Stand was fully inspected, it was still unclear how the fighting had gone down.

Last Stand Hill

What the Americans did find was gruesome. One popular portrayal of the battle was that some of Custer's men had created breastwork fortifications out of dead horses, and though archaeological and historical evidence doesn't substantiate it, there is no question that the cavalry certainly would've taken desperate measures to defend themselves. The legend about using horses as a barricade may have come about because of the fact horses were some of the only corpses intact. Most of the dead cavalrymen had been ritually mutilated and stripped of their clothes and belongings, decomposing to such an extent that many of them could not be identified. The only known survivor in Custer's force was Comanche, the horse of Captain Keogh, who for years afterwards accompanied the 7th Cavalry saddled but riderless.

Custer had been wounded in the arm and shot in the left chest and left temple, both fatal wounds. It's believed that he died before being shot in the head, which probably came as the warriors began finishing off the wounded. Some Indian accounts claimed Custer committed suicide, and though it's believed that some of the 7th U.S. cavalrymen on Last Stand Hill did so, Custer's wounds suggested he did not. Suicide also was not in keeping with a man who had so bravely and recklessly led men throughout his military career.

How did Custer's fighting actually go down? According to the Lakota oral legends, shortly after Sitting Bull returned to the camp, a line of gray cavalry horses bearing Custer's troopers appeared on the crest of a nearby ridge. As the Chief watched, Custer's men charged into the valley toward the encampment, only to quickly find about two thousand Lakota, Teton, and Cheyenne warriors, jubilant after routing the Reno force, appear on his flanks and begin to overwhelm the cavalry troopers. Sitting Bull watched as his vision became reality; Custer's troopers were shattered and soon retreated to a low rise to attempt a final defense. Though it's often called Custer's Last Stand, archaeological evidence suggests the battle seems to have degenerated into a series of running battles in which U.S. troopers – trying to escape to a nearby ravine – were systematically run down by mounted Lakota, Teton, and Cheyenne warriors. Army troops, surveying the scene shortly after the battle, found no piles of rotting horse carcasses as would be expected from a troop or squadron of cavalry killing it horses in defense. The cavalry troopers probably had no time to do so and were more likely enveloped by a force that outnumbered them ten to one. It seems likely that the isolated pockets of Custer's men were surrounded by warriors that prevented them from linking up together as they retreated.

According to Native American accounts passed down by oral legends and survivors of the fighting, Custer's unit was destroyed in less than half an hour, "as long as it takes a hungry man to eat a meal." Those accounts also credited Crazy Horse with personally leading one of the groups of warriors against Custer's unit, taking them by surprise with a charge from the northeast that sent them into a full-fledged rout that the Natives likened to a "buffalo run". If so, it means Crazy Horse was literally all over the field that day, having led his warriors against at least two of the three U.S. Army columns. Some Native accounts recalled this segment of the fight as a "buffalo run."

Along with Crazy Horse, Chief Gall was the other main war leaders that day, while Sitting Bull was more of a spiritual and inspirational participant. Gall especially has been recently credited for his situational and combat awareness, ordering several shifts of Native American warriors that ensured their decisive victory. Interestingly, Gall later claimed Custer's men never got near the river, thus offering a completely different version of events than traditional accounts of the fighting.

How Custer met his fate, and whether there was even a Last Stand, remain subjects of debate. But what is known is that the Battle of the Little Bighorn was one of the U.S. military's biggest debacles. All told, the 7th Cavalry suffered over 50% casualties, with over 250 men killed and over 50 wounded. The dead included Custer's brothers Boston and Thomas, his brother-in-law James Calhoun, and his nephew Henry Reed. Custer and his men were buried where they fell. A year later, Custer's remains (or more accurately, the remains found in the spot labeled with his name) were relocated to West Point for final interment.

The engagement at the Little Bighorn River can be viewed as a failure by Custer to fully appreciate the military capabilities of the Lakota and Cheyenne warriors. Custer may have believed that the Native Americans were already escaping and planned to take Native American women and children hostage. Like Crook, his experience told him that Plains warriors refused to risk harm to their wives and children. His hastily-made battle plan was sound; he planned to use a feint (led by Reno) to draw the warriors attention, while he would lead the true attack. The one problem was the fact that Custer had bad information; it's likely he believed that there were no more that 800 Native Americans in the camp. That number only represents the number considered "non-reservation Indians" who were either with Sitting Bull or had come to join him. Also, many Native American accounts indicate that most of the warriors were sleeping-in on the morning of the attack, likely making the camp misleadingly quiet. Finally, by attacking with his small force, Custer's tactical approach leads most historians to believe he was more interested in keeping the Native Americans from escaping rather than actually engaging them in battle.

The Sioux and other tribes were masters of guerilla warfare and some officers forwarded the idea of adopting the tactics they used, but the idea never moved past the discussion phase. As related in the description of the Fetterman Fight above, the Native American warriors and their leaders both understood and exploited the over-confidence of U.S. military officers and troops. While fighting the "Indian Wars," the nineteenth-century U.S. Army was engaged in an unconventional war, yet it was led and directed by officers with very conventional military training and histories. The prevailing military attitude toward the Native American resistance throughout the West was that it would all soon be over, but the conflict lasted for about 100 years.

The fundamental goal of U.S. policy was the elimination of the hazard and impediment to white settlement throughout the West represented by the presence of Native American tribes. For the U.S. Army, the warrior societies among various Native American tribes constituted well-organized, well-led, motivated, cohesive, and efficient military forces. Among light cavalry formations of the 19th century, Sioux warriors were considered among the best, largely because of their intimate knowledge of and familiarity with their environment.

Initially, many U.S. Army officers considered Native American warriors of all stripes savages and often suffered for failing to appreciate their war leaders' tactical understanding and combat experience. Native American warriors progressed through a series of stages throughout their lives and were analogous to the Japanese Samurai in that their primary "occupation" as men was "warrior/hunter." Young, inexperienced men were trained and mentored by older men, their fathers or male relatives. As men aged they might switch roles and take different paths. As an example, at the Battle of the Little Bighorn River in summer of 1876, Sitting Bull, who had been a fierce and fearless warrior as a younger man, was now operating as a Holy Man and advisor whose main role seems to have been planning the battle and mentoring those participating. Older warriors, it seems, had won their glory and status and were capable of allowing younger warriors – still eager to "count coup" upon their enemies – the chance to earn their own standing and honor. During Little Bighorn, Sitting Bull concerned himself with the safety of the women and children and declined to join the battle with Custer's men, saying, "there were plenty of warriors to meet them."

Sioux warriors' military prowess displayed itself in service to the United States as well. Officers who worked with Native Americans serving as Scouts for the Army found them to be reliable, honest, and disciplined. For most warriors, the transition to working for the Army was a positive one, at least in the short term. With their traditional methods of gaining status among their people (hunting and combat with tribal enemies) effectively eliminated, young warriors adopted the role of Scout as an honorable way of earning distinction and prestige. Usually, these troops were employed as screening forces for larger, regular Army formations. Often, traditional enmity between some of the tribes was exploited for the advantage of the U.S. Army. For instance, while pursuing Sioux warriors, General Crook employed Crow and Shoshone Scouts, traditional enemies of the Sioux, and during the Battle of Rosebud Creek, those Scouts saved Crook's column from being destroyed. From the beginning, however, U.S. military officials failed to understand the "language" of Native American warfare and did not understand how the Sioux viewed the hoards of white settlers traipsing across their lands.

Chapter 5: The Aftermath of Little Bighorn

Sitting Bull's Wakan vision was fulfilled; numerous "blue coats" had been killed, and they lay dead in the greasy grass, like so many dead grass-hoppers. After the Battle of the Little Bighorn, the massive Teton, Lakota, and Cheyenne warrior-army disbanded, and in many ways, the battle, despite being a huge victory for the Native Americans, represented a portent of the coming destruction of the Native American warrior societies and their associated cultures.

In the aftermath of the 7th Cavalry's decimation and the complete destruction of Custer's force, the American public was incensed. The people's ire was probably inflamed by the fact that news reached the eastern United States just as the nation was celebrating its centennial. The nation's reaction was inflammatory and largely reflected the attitudes of the commanders in the field. U.S. troopers had assumed their own inherent eugenic and military superiority over Native Americans and had fully bought into the idea of "manifest destiny." In the months following this battle, the single greatest Native American victory against U.S. troops, the U.S. military sent thousands of cavalry troopers into the region seeking revenge for the "Custer Massacre." Native Americans involved in the battle referred to it as the Battle of the Greasy Grass, referring to the area where the fight happened.

Perhaps realizing that the Army would launch reprisals against them, the huge Native American camp disbanded and scattered. The response the Native Americans feared came quickly, and soon U.S. troops were flooding into Lakota territory. Sitting Bull, ever the tactical leader, knew the end was near and, refusing to surrender, led his people north. Eventually (by May of 1877), he led his people across the border and into Canada, which he called the home of the "Great Mother," referring to Queen Victoria. General Terry, the Chief's one-time military rival, ventured north and offered Sitting Bull surrender terms, but the Chief angrily sent him away.

Meanwhile, others, including Crazy Horse, continued to remain defiant. In early September, Captain Anson Mills and about 150 troopers from the 3rd Cavalry Regiment located a village of about three dozen Cheyenne lodges led by American Horse and attacked it the following morning. The Lakota who escaped the battle fled and warned nearby villages, including one where Crazy Horse and 600 to 800 warriors were living. The fleeing Native Americans said they had been attacked by 100 to 150 troops.

The warriors, a mixture of Sans Arc, Brule, Oglala, and other warriors, rallied behind Crazy Horse's leadership and quickly rode the ten miles to the Cheyenne village, but unbeknownst to the approaching warriors, General George Crook and the remainder of the 3rd Cavalry Regiment had moved into the village. When the approaching warriors reached high ground that allowed them to see the village, they saw an unexpectedly large number of soldiers.

Nevertheless, the warriors opened fire on the soldiers, who quickly formed a defensive perimeter. Crook sent forward a strong line of skirmishers spearheaded by four companies of infantry and followed by three companies of dismounted cavalry troopers. Crazy Horse and his fellow warriors were eventually driven from the high ground and forced to retreat by the determined attack, after which the soldiers burned the village and recovered a number of artifacts from the Battle of the Little Big Horn, including a 7th Cavalry guidon (Company I), gauntlets that had belonged to Captain Myles Keough, weapons, and ammunition. Additionally, the troopers captured over 100 ponies and a cache of dried meat that was distributed to Crook's ill and injured men (Crook's column had been on what they called their "starvation march"). Crazy Horse and his fellow warriors continued to harass the U.S. column for the next few days, but Crook and his men reached the relief of a supply column by mid-September.

The 4th Cavalry Regiment, commanded by Colonel Ranald Mackenzie, was reassigned to the Department of the Platte and moved into the area, and in October of 1876, the regiment departed from Camp Robinson in search of northern Native American villages. By late November, Mackenzie was leading a force of about 1,000 soldiers composed of troopers from the 2nd, 3rd, and 5th Cavalry Regiment in addition to the 4th Cavalry Regiment. The cavalry column was also accompanied by a large contingent of Pawnee and Arapaho scouts, and the force soon located a Cheyenne village of about 170 lodges, led by Dull Knife. The Native Americans were celebrating long into the night, so Mackenzie waited until dawn to attack. His initial thrust pushed many warriors into the frigid countryside without clothes or buffalo robes, but they quickly rallied and began to put up a stiff resistance. Eventually, the Cheyenne were forced to withdraw and the entire village and all its contents were burned. Most of the Cheyenne surrendered, but some refused and joined Crazy Horse and his band's camp. The Dull Knife Fight, as the encounter is known, effectively ended organized Cheyenne resistance to U.S. encroachment.

Red Cloud had refused to openly participate in the Battles of the Rosebud Creek and the Little Big Horn River in 1876, though warriors loyal to him and his son participated in both battles. His role now was largely that of a counselor for the younger warriors, and as an advisor with the other older leaders. But one morning in October 1876, Colonel Mackenzie's troops surrounded

Red Cloud and his followers, forcing their surrender. The warriors were disarmed and dismounted, and the entire band was moved to Fort Robinson, Nebraska. To add to his humiliation and shame, U.S. government officials named Spotted Tail – who had surrendered some time earlier – as the chief of Red Cloud's band. His followers however, refused to accept any other leadership.

Crazy Horse's camp, located on the Tongue River (near present-day Birney, Montana), was populated by about 3,500 Lakota and Cheyenne peoples and included survivors of the Dull Knife Fight. Approaching Crazy Horse's camp was General Nelson Miles, who had driven Sitting Bull and his band into Canada in December of 1876. Seeing the condition of the Cheyenne survivors and considering the approach of winter, Crazy Horse had decided to attempt to negotiate the surrender of his band. However, the delegation he sent to inform Army officers of his pending surrender was attacked and killed by overzealous Army Crow scouts. This action greatly angered Crazy Horse, and he decided that revenge was necessary.

Nelson Miles

Thus, the war chief began a series of raids against Army outposts in an effort to draw General Miles away from his post. Miles led a mixed force of cavalry, infantry, and artillery into the Wolf Mountain area and set up a defensive perimeter on a ridgeline in three feet of snow. Early on the morning of January 8, 1877, Crazy Horse and Two Moons led a force of about 500 warriors in attacks on the soldiers' perimeter. Skillfully using his artillery and superior firepower, Miles was able to frustrate the repeated Native American attacks. Additionally, Miles was able to shift his reserves to cover his flanks when the warriors attempted to outflank his line.

The General then ordered an advance and seized a ridge that allowed him to attack Native American positions with his artillery. Throughout the battle, the weather gradually grew worse, and soon Crazy Horse and his warriors withdrew.

Though the battle was indecisive, it was the last major engagement of the Great Sioux War of 1876-77. Also, the battle showed that Native American settlements were vulnerable to the U.S. Army even in the harsh conditions of the Plains winter. Over the next few months, Native Americans who had been following Crazy Horse began slipping away and returning to their reservations. Throughout the winter, Crazy Horse's people struggled, and by May of 1877, the weary leader led his people to the Red Cloud Agency near Fort Robinson, Nebraska, to surrender.

Chapter 6: The Wounded Knee Massacre and Modern Sioux History

"Our only safety depends upon the total extermination of the Indians. Having wronged them for centuries, we had better, in order to protect our civilization, follow it up by one more wrong and wipe these untamed and untamable creatures from the face of the earth. In this lies future safety for our settlers and the soldiers who are under incompetent commands. Otherwise, we may expect future years to be as full of trouble with the redskins as those have been in the past." – L. Frank Baum, author of *The Wonderful Wizard of Oz*

The Wounded Knee Massacre was the last armed engagement between Sioux warriors and the U.S. military, and it marked the end of effective resistance by any Sioux bands. In late December of 1890, a group of roughly 350 Lakota led by Big Foot and Spotted Elk were escorted to the Wounded Knee Creek area and ordered to establish a camp there. One of the few remaining holy men among the Miniconjou band was advocating violent resistance and repeating the assertion – created and perpetuated by the Ghost Dance movement – that the dyed buckskin Ghost Dance Shirts many wore were impervious to bullets. Fearing another possible uprising despite the fact the band was comprised mostly of women, about 500 U.S. Army troops from the 7th Cavalry Regiment led by Major Samuel M. Whiteside approached the Lakota encampment on the morning of December 29, 1890, with orders to disarm and escort the Native Americans to a railhead for transport to Omaha, Nebraska. Some of the men in the 7th Cavalry had also been part of the 7th Cavalry at Little Bighorn; there could not have been a worse command to send on a mission that required interacting with the Lakota.

The Cavalry Troopers were also supported by four Hotchkiss guns, emplaced on a hill near the Lakota encampment. The Hotchkiss gun was a light artillery piece capable of rapid fire, and when used in a direct fire mode it was devastating.

As the troopers entered the encampment, a shot rang out. It is unclear who fired, but several versions of the cause exist. One states that a trooper tried to disarm a male Lakota named Black Coyote, not knowing he was deaf. The hearing-impaired man and the Trooper struggled over a weapon and the weapon discharged. Another version says that a startled trooper fired inadvertently. Regardless, the single shot triggered a fusillade from the Army troops, including fire from the Hotchkiss guns. One of the Army soldiers, Captain Edward Godfrey, explained, "I know the men did not aim deliberately and they were greatly excited. I don't believe they saw their sights. They fired rapidly but it seemed to me only a few seconds till there was not a living thing before us; warriors, squaws, children, ponies, and dogs ... went down before that unaimed fire." Hugh McGinnis, another 7th Cavalry soldier, wrote, "General Nelson A. Miles who visited the scene of carnage, following a three day blizzard, estimated that around 300 snow shrouded forms were strewn over the countryside. He also discovered to his horror that helpless children and women with babes in their arms had been chased as far as two miles from the original scene of encounter and cut down without mercy by the troopers. ... Judging by the slaughter on the battlefield it was suggested that the soldiers simply went berserk. For who could explain such a merciless disregard for life? ... As I see it the battle was more or less a matter of spontaneous combustion, sparked by mutual distrust…"

The resulting assault would eventually kill most of the Native Americans, including both Big Foot and Spotted Elk. Approximately 30 U.S. Army soldiers were killed and about 40 were wounded, nearly all struck by friendly fire in the chaotic, close-quarters shooting. Of the Native American dead, most were killed outright, but the wounded were left on the frozen ground to perish during the frigid night. The following day, the frozen bodies – which had been stripped by the soldiers for souvenirs – were buried in mass grave.

One of the Oglala Lakota present at Wounded Knee, a medicine man named Black Elk, described the massacre, "I did not know then how much was ended. When I look back now from this high hill of my old age, I can still see the butchered women and children lying heaped and scattered all along the crooked gulch as plain as when I saw them with eyes young. And I can see that something else died there in the bloody mud, and was buried in the blizzard. A people's dream died there. It was a beautiful dream ... the nation's hoop is broken and scattered. There is no center any longer, and the sacred tree is dead." The famous Oglala chief American Horse added, "There was a woman with an infant in her arms who was killed as she almost touched the flag of truce ... A mother was shot down with her infant; the child not knowing that its mother was dead was still nursing ... The women as they were fleeing with their babies were killed together, shot right through ... and after most all of them had been killed a cry was made that all those who were not killed or wounded should come forth and they would be safe. Little boys ... came out of their places of refuge, and as soon as they came in sight a number of soldiers surrounded them and butchered them there."

The Wounded Knee Massacre had several outcomes. The soldiers who participated in the massacre were commended and awarded for their actions, with 20 of them receiving the nation's highest military award, the Congressional Medal of Honor, for action during the "battle." When news spread about the events at Wounded Knee, it became clear to its adherents that the Ghost

Dance had failed to live up to its promises. The decorated buckskin Ghost Dance shirts had failed to stop bullets, and, more disappointingly, the dead warriors and the buffalo had failed to return. Since the predictions of Wovoka (the original Ghost Dance prophet) proved false, the practice quickly disappeared, though some remained faithful to its outlandish claims. Isolated pockets of believers continued to carry on a version of the faith, but it was greatly diminished in terms of promising a return of the traditional plains horse culture. Shoshone Ghost Dancers performed the last known examples of the Ghost Dance rituals during the 1950s.

The Wounded Knee Massacre would grow to become a source of inspiration for a generation of Sioux people who came of age in the 1960s, and they sought to reestablish negotiations with the United States as a sovereign and independent nation. The American Indian Movement would engage in confrontational and at times violent resistance to perceived U.S. government oppression at Alcatraz, the Bureau of Indian Affairs building in Washington D.C., and later the town of Wounded Knee, South Dakota, and the Wounded Knee Massacre site.

The American Indian Movement was founded in Minneapolis, Minnesota, in 1968. Established by a group of some 200 Sioux, Ojibwa, and other indigenous people, the movement coalesced as a response to ongoing cycles of poverty, racism, and despair prevalent among Native American people. Among the primary targets of the fledgling organization was the Bureau of Indian Affairs, which they felt had waged a virtual culture war against Native Americans by proclaiming that everything related to traditional practices, including hair length and spiritual beliefs, must be driven from the reservation system and Native Americans themselves. In response to this attitude, members of the original movement seized upon Native Americans' biggest assets: their spiritual beliefs and their intimate connection to the land. From the beginning, the movement claimed to be oriented to the traditional religious beliefs of Native Americans. In order to be fully bona fide members of the organization, Native Americans must participate in the Sun Dance ritual held at the Pine Ridge Reservation.

Initially, the movement based its organization on existing, urban civil rights groups but soon began to forge its own identity based upon traditional beliefs. According to Leonard Peltier, who would become and remains a notorious and controversial figure for allegedly murdering two FBI officials, the American Indian Movement (AIM) never went "any place without being asked by the chiefs and elders; we have never gone any place without the medicine man." The movement pressured the bureaucracy conducting the "War on Poverty," hoping to increase Native American influence on decision-making that affects indigenous people, in an effort to help Native Americans protect themselves from abuse law enforcement and the federal government. The movement tried to avoid entangling itself in local and tribal politics but was prevailed upon by Native Americans living on reservations in an attempt to gain legal justice for elderly Native Americans. AIM soon found itself responding to indigenous people's requests and supporting Native American causes.

In the November of 1969, a beacon from Ghirardelli Square in San Francisco, California, flashed a message repeatedly toward Alcatraz Island: "Go Indians!" A coalition of Native Americans – including Sioux people – had seized the former island prison and would occupy the site for roughly 18 months, from November 1969 until June 1971. The Native American occupiers of the former maximum security prison stated the purpose of the their occupation was to bring attention to the refusal of the U.S. government to honor treaties signed in the 19th century and to improve the treatment of Native American with regard to human rights. Modoc and Hopi tribal members had been incarcerated in the island prison, which was itself seized by the U.S. government from the Ohone tribe of northern California, who believed the island was a place occupied by evil spirits and used it as a place of banishment and isolation for tribal members. The Ohone also plied the island's resources, gathering ocean borne foodstuffs and sea-bird eggs, regardless of its supposed "evil spirits." Eventually, U.S. Federal Marshals forcibly removed the Native American occupiers from the island, and although the AIM had failed to achieve its immediate goal of returning the island to Native American ownership, the Movement did succeed in bringing attention to the plight of Native Americans in the United States.

In August 1972, Brule Sioux tribal leader Robert Burnette conceived the idea of a march to Washington D.C., dubbing the protest "The Trail of Broken Treaties". The plan was to present a set of 20 requests to Bureau of Indian Affairs officials with the hope of addressing past and present injustices suffered by indigenous people in the United States. Among these requests was the restoration of constitutional treaty-making authority, the establishment of a treaty commission to make new treaties with Native American tribes, land reform and restoration of a 110 million acres native land base, and the creation of a commission to review treaty commitments and violations. By October, a caravan of Native Americans representing some 300 tribes from the United States and Canada was traveling across the country in what became known as "The Trail of Broken Treaties Caravan". The Caravan deliberately retraced the route of the infamous "Trail of Tears" to call attention to the continuing mistreatment of indigenous peoples by the U.S. government.

When the Caravan arrived in Washington D.C., its members were met by a large group of Native Americans prepared to join the protest, bringing the total number of indigenous protesters to over 2,000. Officials dispatched riot police, and as the protesters began to leave the Bureau of Indian Affairs building, the police began pushing them out. In the spur of the moment, fearing the protesters might be brutalized by the riot police, AIM leaders urged the protesters to run back into the Bureau of Indian building. Despite police attempts to enter the building, the indigenous protesters occupied the building for six days, doing an estimated $700,000 in damage and destroying land records, treaties, and other documents. The protesters also seized numerous confidential Bureau documents that revealed questionable government practices regarding reservation land and mineral rights. On November 9, 1972, a resolution was reached stating that no protesters would be prosecuted for their actions during the occupation, $66,000 dollars would be awarded to the protesters to pay for their return travel, and the 20 requests would be considered. In early January 1973, the Nixon administration disappointed the protesters by dismissing the 20 requests and dashing Native American hopes for true self-determination.

Native American dissatisfaction with government oversight and policies would come to a head with what is sometimes referred to as the final battle over the Fort Laramie Treaty of 1868: the Wounded Knee Siege. In the months leading up to the siege, civil unrest fomented among the Oglala Lakota Sioux living on the Pine Ridge Reservation. The division on the reservation was between traditional Lakota people who wanted less intrusion and governance from the federal government and the "official" tribal leaders, especially tribal president Richard Wilson. A grass roots effort to impeach Wilson, who many Oglala regarded as corrupt and abusive, failed, further exacerbating the situation. The "Traditionals" were Oglala who maintained their language and traditional religious beliefs, while Wilson and his faction were composed of government supporters. An additional issue for the Traditionals was Wilson's mixed race background and his perceived nepotism; full-blooded Oglala felt they were passed over when considered for the few jobs or other opportunities on the reservation. Strip-mining on tribal land and the associated exposure to chemicals used in the process were becoming problems, causing illness and birth defects with alarmingly frequency. Wilson and his administration encouraged the strip-mining and advocated for the official sale of the Black Hills to the federal government, and many Oglala viewed Wilson and the tribal government as pawns of the Bureau of Indian Affairs. Opposition to Wilson, who had rapidly become an autocrat after his 1972 election, was met with violent response from his personal militia called the Guardians of Our Oglala Nation. In late February of 1973, AIM set up an open meeting to discuss the situation. According to AIM accounts, almost immediately after their arrival in Wounded Knee, government official set up roadblocks and isolated the town.

News of the occupation quickly spread, and soon members of some 75 Native American nations arrived on the scene to stand in solidarity with the Oglala Traditionals. U.S. federal Marshals and members of the National Guard attempted to seal off Wounded Knee, but daily, additional protesters were able to sneak through the lines to join the occupiers. The standoff lasted for 71 days, during which AIM members reiterated several requests from their recent Bureau of Indian Affairs occupation including a call for an examination of over 370 treaties between Native American tribes and the U.S. government. The warriors also called for a Senate Committee to investigate the action of the Department of the Interior and the Bureau of Indian Affairs and the two agencies' handling of Oglala tribal affairs.

Meanwhile, the confrontation became increasingly violent with daily exchanges of heavy gunfire between the occupiers and Marshals and National Guard troops. During the course of the siege, two Native Americans were killed outright and one U.S. Marshal was paralyzed by gunfire and later died from complications. U.S. officials cut electricity to the town and tightened the perimeter, but volunteers continued to sneak backpack loads of food and supplies in to the occupiers. Twelve of these backpackers were captured by members of Wilson's militia and disappeared, likely murdered. A cursory investigation was conducted by U.S. government but was quickly called off and no further inquiry into the disappearances was made. After seventy-one days occupying Wounded Knee, AIM and its supporters surrendered, and U.S. government official made over 1,200 arrests.

In the years following the AIM siege of Wounded Knee, tensions mounted at the Pine Ridge Reservation, stoking the flames between Native Americans, the FBI, and the Bureau of Indian Affairs. In the three years after the occupation, 64 tribal members were the victims of unsolved murders, and some 300 were harassed and beaten. Over 560 arrests were made during these three years, but they resulted in only 15 convictions. For the Oglala, the period following the occupation had been harsh, but they had proven that they were a proud and courageous people, willing to face adversity and intimidation. And they remained hopeful and ultimately triumphant.